EMMANUEL JOSEPH

The Metamorphosis of Well-being, Synchronizing Wellness, Financial Stability, and Emotional Depth

Copyright © 2025 by Emmanuel Joseph

All rights reserved. No part of this publication may be reproduced, stored or transmitted in any form or by any means, electronic, mechanical, photocopying, recording, scanning, or otherwise without written permission from the publisher. It is illegal to copy this book, post it to a website, or distribute it by any other means without permission.

First edition

This book was professionally typeset on Reedsy.
Find out more at reedsy.com

Contents

1 Chapter 1: Introduction to Holistic Well-being   1
2 Chapter 2: The Pillar of Physical Wellness   3
3 Chapter 3: Financial Stability as a Foundation   5
4 Chapter 4: The Depths of Emotional Well-being   7
5 Chapter 5: The Interplay of Wellness, Finance, and Emotion   9
6 Chapter 6: Strategies for Integrating Wellness Practices   11
7 Chapter 7: The Role of Mindfulness in Well-being   13
8 Chapter 8: Financial Planning for a Secure Future   15
9 Chapter 9: Building Resilience through Emotional...   17
10 Chapter 10: The Power of Positive Habits   19
11 Chapter 11: The Importance of Community and Support   21
12 Chapter 12: Navigating Life Transitions with Grace   23
13 Chapter 13: The Role of Gratitude in Well-being   25
14 Chapter 14: Balancing Work and Personal Life   27
15 Chapter 15: Embracing a Life of Purpose and Fulfillment   29

1

Chapter 1: Introduction to Holistic Well-being

The concept of holistic well-being revolves around the integration of physical wellness, financial stability, and emotional depth. These elements are intricately connected, creating a balanced and harmonious life when synchronized. Physical wellness provides the energy and vitality needed to pursue life's goals, while financial stability offers the security and peace of mind to focus on other aspects of well-being. Emotional depth enhances our relationships and enriches our overall experience, making life more meaningful.

When these three pillars are in harmony, they support and enhance one another. Physical wellness can improve mental clarity and emotional resilience, making it easier to manage financial responsibilities. In turn, financial stability reduces stress and allows for better focus on health and emotional growth. Emotional depth fosters strong relationships and a sense of purpose, motivating individuals to maintain their physical and financial well-being. By viewing well-being as a holistic concept, we can create a more fulfilling and balanced life.

The importance of holistic well-being cannot be overstated in today's fast-paced world. Many people focus on one or two aspects of their well-being, neglecting others. This imbalance can lead to burnout, stress, and dissatisfaction. By recognizing the interconnectedness of physical, financial, and emotional health, we can create a more sustainable and satisfying approach to well-being. This chapter sets the stage for exploring each of these pillars in greater depth, providing practical strategies for achieving balance and harmony.

Ultimately, holistic well-being is about creating a life that is rich in all aspects. It involves nurturing our bodies, managing our finances wisely, and cultivating emotional intelligence. By doing so, we can enjoy a higher quality of life, marked by vitality, security, and deep connections. This book will guide you through the process of achieving holistic well-being, offering insights and tools to help you synchronize wellness, financial stability, and emotional depth.

2

Chapter 2: The Pillar of Physical Wellness

Physical wellness is the foundation upon which all other aspects of well-being are built. It encompasses not only the absence of illness but also the presence of positive health behaviors, such as regular exercise, balanced nutrition, and adequate rest. By prioritizing physical wellness, we can enhance our energy levels, improve our mental clarity, and increase our overall quality of life. This chapter delves into the key components of physical wellness and provides practical tips for incorporating healthy habits into our daily routines.

Regular exercise is a cornerstone of physical wellness, offering numerous benefits for both the body and mind. It helps to maintain a healthy weight, reduce the risk of chronic diseases, and improve cardiovascular health. Exercise also releases endorphins, which boost mood and reduce stress. This chapter explores various types of physical activity, from aerobic exercise to strength training, and offers guidance on creating a personalized fitness plan that aligns with your goals and lifestyle.

Balanced nutrition is another critical aspect of physical wellness. A well-rounded diet provides the essential nutrients needed for optimal functioning and helps to prevent illness. This chapter discusses the importance of consuming a variety of whole foods, including fruits, vegetables, lean proteins, and healthy fats. It also addresses common dietary challenges, such as portion control and mindful eating, and offers strategies for making healthier food choices. By nourishing our bodies with the right nutrients, we can support our overall health and well-being.

Adequate rest and recovery are essential components of physical wellness. Sleep plays a crucial role in maintaining physical and mental health, as it allows the body to repair and rejuvenate. This chapter highlights the importance of establishing healthy sleep habits, such as maintaining a consistent sleep schedule and creating a restful sleep environment. It also addresses the impact of stress on sleep quality and offers techniques for managing stress to promote better rest. By prioritizing rest and recovery, we can enhance our physical wellness and overall well-being.

3

Chapter 3: Financial Stability as a Foundation

Financial stability is a bedrock of well-being, providing the security necessary to focus on other areas of life. It involves understanding and managing one's finances, ensuring that income exceeds expenses, and preparing for future needs. This chapter delves into the importance of budgeting, saving, and investing as essential components of financial stability. It also emphasizes the significance of financial literacy and its role in making informed decisions that lead to long-term security and prosperity.

Budgeting is a fundamental practice for achieving financial stability. It involves creating a plan for income and expenses, ensuring that spending aligns with financial goals. This chapter discusses various budgeting methods, such as the 50/30/20 rule, and offers practical tips for tracking expenses and adjusting spending habits. By maintaining a well-structured budget, individuals can gain control over their finances and make informed decisions that support their overall well-being.

Saving is another crucial aspect of financial stability. It provides a safety net for unexpected expenses and enables individuals to achieve their long-term goals. This chapter explores different saving strategies, such as building an emergency fund, setting aside money for specific goals, and taking advantage of employer-sponsored retirement plans. It also highlights the importance of automating savings to ensure consistency. By prioritizing saving, individuals can create a financial cushion that offers peace of mind and security.

Investing is a powerful tool for building wealth and achieving financial stability. This chapter discusses the basics of investing, including the different types of investments, such as stocks, bonds, and real estate. It also covers the principles of risk and return, diversification, and the importance of a long-term perspective. By understanding and implementing sound investment strategies, individuals can grow their wealth and create a stable financial future that supports their overall well-being.

4

Chapter 4: The Depths of Emotional Well-being

Emotional well-being is the heartbeat of a fulfilling life, influencing our relationships, decision-making, and overall happiness. It involves understanding and managing our emotions, developing resilience, and fostering positive relationships. This chapter delves into the significance of emotional intelligence, self-awareness, and self-regulation. It also discusses the impact of positive and negative emotions on our mental health and offers strategies for managing stress and cultivating emotional balance.

Emotional intelligence is the ability to recognize, understand, and manage our own emotions, as well as the emotions of others. This chapter explores the components of emotional intelligence, including self-awareness, self-regulation, motivation, empathy, and social skills. It discusses how developing emotional intelligence can enhance our relationships, improve decision-making, and increase overall life satisfaction. By building emotional intelligence, individuals can navigate life's challenges with greater ease and resilience.

Self-awareness is a key aspect of emotional well-being, enabling individuals to understand their thoughts, feelings, and behaviors. This chapter discusses the importance of self-reflection and mindfulness in developing self-awareness. It offers practical exercises, such as journaling and meditation, to help individuals gain insight into their emotions and identify patterns that may impact their well-being. By cultivating self-awareness, individuals can make more conscious choices and improve their overall emotional health.

Managing stress is essential for maintaining emotional well-being. This chapter explores the various sources of stress and their impact on mental and physical health. It offers strategies for managing stress, such as developing healthy coping mechanisms, setting boundaries, and practicing relaxation techniques. By effectively managing stress, individuals can enhance their emotional resilience and overall well-being, leading to a more balanced and fulfilling life.

5

Chapter 5: The Interplay of Wellness, Finance, and Emotion

The interconnectedness of physical wellness, financial stability, and emotional well-being forms a symbiotic relationship that enhances our overall quality of life. This chapter examines how these elements influence and support one another, creating a holistic approach to well-being. It explores the ripple effects of financial stress on physical health and emotional stability, as well as the benefits of a balanced lifestyle on financial decision-making.

Financial stress can have a significant impact on physical health, leading to issues such as insomnia, headaches, and weakened immune function. This chapter discusses the physiological effects of financial stress and offers strategies for mitigating its impact. By addressing financial concerns and creating a stable financial foundation, individuals can reduce stress and improve their overall physical health. This holistic approach to well-being emphasizes the importance of financial stability in maintaining a healthy lifestyle.

Emotional well-being also plays a crucial role in financial decision-making. Individuals who are emotionally balanced and self-aware are better equipped to make thoughtful and informed financial choices. This chapter explores the influence of emotions on spending habits, saving behaviors, and investment decisions. It offers practical tips for managing emotions in the context of financial planning, such as setting realistic goals and seeking professional advice. By fostering emotional well-being, individuals can make sound financial decisions that support their overall well-being.

The benefits of a balanced lifestyle extend beyond physical and emotional health, positively impacting financial stability. This chapter discusses how regular exercise, proper nutrition, and adequate rest can improve focus, decision-making, and productivity. It also highlights the importance of maintaining a healthy work-life balance to prevent burnout and ensure long-term financial success. By integrating wellness practices into their daily routines, individuals can create a harmonious and fulfilling life that supports all aspects of well-being.

6

Chapter 6: Strategies for Integrating Wellness Practices

Incorporating wellness practices into our daily routines is essential for achieving holistic well-being. This chapter offers practical strategies for integrating physical, financial, and emotional wellness into our lives. It discusses the importance of setting realistic goals, creating a balanced schedule, and maintaining consistency. By adopting these practices, we can cultivate a harmonious and fulfilling lifestyle.

Setting realistic goals is the first step towards integrating wellness practices into our daily lives. This chapter explores the process of goal-setting, emphasizing the importance of creating specific, measurable, achievable, relevant, and time-bound (SMART) goals. It offers guidance on breaking down larger goals into smaller, manageable steps and tracking progress. By setting realistic goals, individuals can create a clear path towards achieving holistic well-being.

Creating a balanced schedule is crucial for incorporating wellness practices into our daily routines. This chapter discusses the importance of time management and prioritization in achieving a balanced lifestyle. It offers practical tips for organizing daily activities, such as allocating time for exercise, relaxation, and social connections. By creating a balanced schedule, individuals can ensure that all aspects of well-being are addressed and maintained.

Maintaining consistency is key to the successful integration of wellness practices. This chapter explores the role of habits in achieving long-term well-being and offers strategies for building and maintaining positive habits. It discusses the importance of routine and repetition in establishing new behaviors and provides tips for staying motivated and overcoming obstacles. By maintaining consistency, individuals can create lasting changes that support their overall well-being.

This chapter also highlights the importance of self-compassion and flexibility in the pursuit of well-being. It encourages individuals to be kind to themselves, recognizing that setbacks and challenges are a natural part of the journey. It offers strategies for adapting wellness practices to changing circumstances and emphasizes the importance of celebrating progress. By embracing self-compassion and flexibility, individuals can create a sustainable and fulfilling approach to holistic well-being.

7

Chapter 7: The Role of Mindfulness in Well-being

Mindfulness is a powerful practice that enhances our awareness and presence in the moment, contributing to our overall well-being. It involves paying attention to our thoughts, feelings, and sensations without judgment, allowing us to experience life more fully. This chapter explores the benefits of mindfulness practices, such as meditation, deep breathing, and mindful movement. By incorporating mindfulness into our daily routines, we can reduce stress, improve focus, and cultivate emotional resilience.

Meditation is one of the most well-known mindfulness practices, offering numerous benefits for both the mind and body. This chapter discusses different types of meditation, such as focused attention, loving-kindness, and body scan meditations. It provides practical tips for beginners, including finding a quiet space, setting a timer, and focusing on the breath. By practicing meditation regularly, individuals can develop greater self-awareness and emotional balance.

Deep breathing is another effective mindfulness technique that can help reduce stress and promote relaxation. This chapter explores various deep breathing exercises, such as diaphragmatic breathing, box breathing, and 4-7-8 breathing. It explains the physiological benefits of deep breathing, including its ability to activate the body's relaxation response. By incorporating deep breathing into our daily routines, we can enhance our overall well-being and manage stress more effectively.

Mindful movement practices, such as yoga and tai chi, combine physical activity with mindfulness, offering a holistic approach to well-being. This chapter discusses the benefits of mindful movement, including improved flexibility, strength, and mental clarity. It offers guidance on incorporating these practices into our lives, whether through attending classes, following online tutorials, or practicing at home. By embracing mindful movement, we can cultivate a greater sense of balance and harmony in our lives.

8

Chapter 8: Financial Planning for a Secure Future

Effective financial planning is essential for achieving long-term stability and security. It involves setting goals, creating a budget, and developing an investment strategy that aligns with one's financial objectives. This chapter delves into the principles of financial planning, offering practical guidance for creating a comprehensive financial plan. By taking a proactive approach to financial planning, individuals can ensure a secure and prosperous future.

Setting financial goals is the first step in creating a financial plan. This chapter discusses the importance of identifying short-term, medium-term, and long-term financial goals. It offers practical tips for setting realistic and achievable goals, such as paying off debt, saving for a down payment on a home, or planning for retirement. By setting clear financial goals, individuals can create a roadmap for their financial future.

Creating a budget is a crucial aspect of financial planning, allowing individuals to manage their income and expenses effectively. This chapter explores different budgeting methods, such as zero-based budgeting and the envelope system. It provides guidance on tracking expenses, reducing unnecessary spending, and allocating funds towards savings and investments. By maintaining a well-structured budget, individuals can gain control over their finances and make informed decisions that support their overall well-being.

Developing an investment strategy is essential for building wealth and achieving long-term financial goals. This chapter discusses the basics of investing, including the different types of investments, such as stocks, bonds, and real estate. It also covers the principles of risk and return, diversification, and the importance of a long-term perspective. By understanding and implementing sound investment strategies, individuals can grow their wealth and create a stable financial future that supports their overall well-being.

9

Chapter 9: Building Resilience through Emotional Intelligence

Emotional intelligence is the ability to recognize, understand, and manage our emotions, as well as the emotions of others. It plays a crucial role in building resilience and navigating life's challenges with grace. This chapter explores the components of emotional intelligence, including self-awareness, self-regulation, motivation, empathy, and social skills. By developing emotional intelligence, individuals can enhance their relationships, improve decision-making, and increase overall life satisfaction.

Self-awareness is the foundation of emotional intelligence, enabling individuals to understand their thoughts, feelings, and behaviors. This chapter discusses the importance of self-reflection and mindfulness in developing self-awareness. It offers practical exercises, such as journaling and meditation, to help individuals gain insight into their emotions and identify patterns that may impact their well-being. By cultivating self-awareness, individuals can make more conscious choices and improve their overall emotional health.

Self-regulation involves managing one's emotions and behaviors in a healthy and productive manner. This chapter explores strategies for self-regulation, such as setting boundaries, practicing relaxation techniques, and developing healthy coping mechanisms. It also discusses the importance of impulse control and delayed gratification in achieving long-term goals. By developing self-regulation skills, individuals can navigate challenges with greater resilience and maintain emotional balance.

Empathy and social skills are essential components of emotional intelligence that enhance our relationships and social interactions. This chapter discusses the importance of understanding and sharing the feelings of others, as well as effective communication and conflict resolution skills. It offers practical tips for developing empathy, such as active listening and perspective-taking. By fostering empathy and social skills, individuals can create deeper and more meaningful connections with others, contributing to their overall well-being.

10

Chapter 10: The Power of Positive Habits

Positive habits are the building blocks of a healthy and fulfilling life. They shape our behaviors, influence our decisions, and contribute to our overall well-being. This chapter examines the impact of habits on our physical, financial, and emotional health. It offers strategies for creating and maintaining positive habits, such as setting clear intentions, tracking progress, and celebrating successes. By cultivating positive habits, we can create a strong foundation for holistic well-being.

Creating positive habits begins with setting clear intentions and identifying the behaviors we want to change or adopt. This chapter discusses the importance of specificity and commitment in habit formation. It provides practical tips for setting realistic goals, breaking down larger habits into smaller, manageable steps, and establishing a routine. By setting clear intentions, individuals can create a roadmap for developing positive habits.

Tracking progress is an essential part of maintaining positive habits. This chapter explores various methods for tracking habits, such as using habit trackers, journals, or apps. It discusses the benefits of monitoring progress, including increased motivation, accountability, and self-awareness. By tracking their habits, individuals can identify patterns, celebrate successes, and make adjustments as needed to stay on track.

Celebrating successes is a crucial aspect of habit formation, reinforcing positive behaviors and motivating individuals to continue their efforts.

This chapter offers strategies for celebrating small wins, such as rewarding oneself, acknowledging progress, and sharing achievements with others. It also discusses the importance of self-compassion and patience in the habit-forming process. By celebrating successes, individuals can maintain motivation and build lasting positive habits.

11

Chapter 11: The Importance of Community and Support

Our well-being is deeply influenced by the relationships and support systems we cultivate. Strong connections with family, friends, and the wider community provide emotional support, a sense of belonging, and opportunities for personal growth. This chapter discusses the importance of building a robust network of relationships and offers strategies for fostering meaningful connections. By nurturing our social ties, we can enhance our overall well-being and create a sense of community.

Family relationships form the core of our support system, providing love, guidance, and stability. This chapter explores the dynamics of family relationships and their impact on well-being. It discusses the importance of communication, mutual respect, and shared experiences in strengthening family bonds. By prioritizing family connections, individuals can create a supportive and nurturing environment that contributes to their emotional and mental health.

Friendships play a crucial role in our well-being, offering companionship, laughter, and emotional support. This chapter examines the benefits of maintaining strong friendships and provides tips for building and sustaining these relationships. It emphasizes the importance of spending quality time with friends, being a good listener, and offering support during difficult times.

By investing in friendships, individuals can create a network of support that enhances their overall well-being.

Community involvement extends our support system beyond family and friends, providing opportunities for social engagement and personal growth. This chapter discusses the benefits of participating in community activities, such as volunteering, joining clubs, or attending local events. It offers guidance on finding and engaging with community organizations that align with one's interests and values. By becoming active members of their communities, individuals can develop a sense of belonging and purpose that contributes to their overall well-being.

12

Chapter 12: Navigating Life Transitions with Grace

Life transitions, such as career changes, relocation, and personal milestones, can have a significant impact on our well-being. These changes often bring challenges, but they also offer opportunities for growth and self-discovery. This chapter offers strategies for navigating life transitions with grace and resilience. By approaching these changes with a positive mindset and practical strategies, individuals can embrace new opportunities and maintain their well-being.

Career changes are a common life transition that can affect our financial stability and emotional well-being. This chapter discusses the challenges and opportunities associated with changing careers, such as adapting to new roles, learning new skills, and building new professional relationships. It offers practical tips for managing career transitions, such as setting clear goals, seeking professional development opportunities, and maintaining a positive attitude. By approaching career changes with resilience, individuals can navigate these transitions successfully and continue to thrive.

Relocation is another significant life transition that can impact well-being. Moving to a new city or country involves adjusting to a new environment, making new connections, and establishing new routines. This chapter explores the emotional and practical aspects of relocation, offering strategies for adapting to a new place, building a support network, and managing the stress associated with moving. By approaching relocation with an open mind and a proactive attitude, individuals can make the transition smoother and more enjoyable.

Personal milestones, such as marriage, parenthood, or retirement, are significant life transitions that bring both joy and challenges. This chapter discusses the impact of these milestones on well-being and offers strategies for navigating them with grace. It emphasizes the importance of preparation, communication, and self-care in managing these changes. By embracing personal milestones with a positive mindset and practical strategies, individuals can enhance their overall well-being and enjoy the journey.

13

Chapter 13: The Role of Gratitude in Well-being

Gratitude is a powerful practice that can enhance our overall well-being and outlook on life. It involves recognizing and appreciating the positive aspects of our lives, which can increase happiness, improve relationships, and foster resilience. This chapter explores the benefits of cultivating gratitude and offers practical tips for incorporating gratitude into our daily routines. By embracing gratitude, individuals can create a more positive and fulfilling life.

The practice of gratitude can significantly improve our mental health and emotional well-being. This chapter discusses the psychological benefits of gratitude, such as increased happiness, reduced stress, and enhanced self-esteem. It explores the science behind gratitude, highlighting research studies that demonstrate its positive effects. By understanding the impact of gratitude on our mental health, individuals can appreciate its importance and make it a regular part of their lives.

Gratitude can also strengthen our relationships by fostering a sense of appreciation and connection. This chapter examines how expressing gratitude can enhance our interactions with others, improve communication, and build stronger bonds. It offers practical tips for showing appreciation to family, friends, and colleagues, such as writing thank-you notes, giving compliments, and acknowledging acts of kindness. By practicing gratitude in our relationships, we can create a more supportive and loving environment.

Incorporating gratitude into our daily routines can help us maintain a positive outlook on life. This chapter provides practical exercises for cultivating gratitude, such as keeping a gratitude journal, practicing mindful gratitude, and reflecting on positive experiences. It discusses the importance of consistency and mindfulness in maintaining a gratitude practice. By integrating gratitude into our daily lives, individuals can enhance their overall well-being and create a more positive and fulfilling life.

14

Chapter 14: Balancing Work and Personal Life

Achieving a balance between work and personal life is essential for holistic well-being. The demands of work can often encroach on personal time, leading to stress and burnout. This chapter discusses the challenges and benefits of maintaining a healthy work-life balance and offers strategies for setting boundaries, managing time effectively, and prioritizing self-care. By creating a balance between work and personal life, individuals can reduce stress and enhance their overall well-being.

Setting boundaries is a crucial step in achieving work-life balance. This chapter explores the importance of establishing clear boundaries between work and personal time, such as setting specific work hours and creating a designated workspace. It offers practical tips for communicating boundaries with employers, colleagues, and family members. By setting and respecting boundaries, individuals can create a healthier balance between work and personal life.

Effective time management is essential for maintaining work-life balance. This chapter discusses various time management techniques, such as prioritizing tasks, using productivity tools, and creating a daily schedule. It emphasizes the importance of allocating time for both work and personal activities, including exercise, hobbies, and social interactions. By managing their time effectively, individuals can ensure that they have time for both work and personal life, reducing stress and increasing overall well-being.

Prioritizing self-care is vital for achieving work-life balance. This chapter explores the importance of self-care practices, such as regular exercise, healthy eating, and relaxation techniques, in maintaining physical and mental health. It offers practical tips for incorporating self-care into daily routines, such as scheduling regular breaks, practicing mindfulness, and setting aside time for leisure activities. By prioritizing self-care, individuals can enhance their well-being and prevent burnout.

15

Chapter 15: Embracing a Life of Purpose and Fulfillment

Living a life of purpose and fulfillment is the ultimate goal of well-being. It involves identifying our passions, setting meaningful goals, and pursuing activities that align with our values. This chapter explores the importance of living with purpose and offers strategies for discovering and embracing one's purpose. By living a purposeful life, individuals can achieve a deep sense of satisfaction and contentment.

Identifying one's passions is the first step towards living a purposeful life. This chapter discusses the importance of self-exploration and reflection in discovering what truly matters to us. It offers practical exercises for identifying passions, such as journaling, exploring new interests, and seeking feedback from others. By understanding their passions, individuals can create a roadmap for living a purposeful and fulfilling life.

Setting meaningful goals is essential for achieving a life of purpose. This chapter explores the process of goal-setting, emphasizing the importance of creating specific, measurable, achievable, relevant, and time-bound (SMART) goals. It offers guidance on breaking down larger goals into smaller, manageable steps and tracking progress. By setting meaningful goals, individuals can create a clear path towards living a purposeful life.

Pursuing activities that align with one's values is crucial for achieving fulfillment. This chapter discusses the importance of aligning actions with values and offers strategies for identifying and prioritizing activities that bring joy and satisfaction. It emphasizes the importance of staying true to oneself and making choices that reflect one's values. By pursuing activities that align with their values, individuals can create a fulfilling and meaningful life.

Living with purpose involves embracing the journey and being open to growth and change. This chapter discusses the importance of adaptability, resilience, and a positive mindset in navigating life's challenges. It offers practical tips for staying motivated, overcoming obstacles, and celebrating progress. By embracing the journey and living with purpose, individuals can achieve a deep sense of fulfillment and well-being.

Book Description:

In *The Metamorphosis of Well-being: Synchronizing Wellness, Financial Stability, and Emotional Depth*, embark on a transformative journey towards achieving a balanced and fulfilling life. This compelling book delves into the intricate interplay between physical health, financial stability, and emotional richness, revealing how their harmonious integration can elevate your overall well-being.

Discover the essential pillars of holistic well-being, starting with the foundation of physical wellness. Learn how to maintain a healthy lifestyle through balanced nutrition, regular exercise, and adequate rest, setting the stage for a vibrant and energetic life. Explore the crucial role of financial stability in providing the security and peace of mind needed to focus on other areas of life. Uncover the principles of sound financial management, including budgeting, saving, and investing, and how these practices can create a stable environment that supports your overall well-being.

Dive into the depths of emotional well-being, the heartbeat of a fulfilling life. Understand the significance of emotional intelligence, self-awareness, and resilience, and how nurturing these aspects can enrich your relationships and decision-making processes. Learn practical strategies for managing stress and cultivating emotional balance, fostering deeper connections and greater contentment.

CHAPTER 15: EMBRACING A LIFE OF PURPOSE AND FULFILLMENT

The Metamorphosis of Well-being offers practical insights and strategies for integrating wellness practices into your daily routines, emphasizing the importance of setting realistic goals, creating a balanced schedule, and maintaining consistency. Explore the power of mindfulness, financial planning, and positive habits in enhancing your overall well-being. Understand the importance of community and support systems, and how meaningful connections can create a sense of belonging and purpose.

Navigate life transitions with grace, embrace the practice of gratitude, and achieve a harmonious work-life balance. This book provides a comprehensive guide to living a life of purpose and fulfillment, helping you identify your passions, set meaningful goals, and pursue activities that align with your values.

Embark on the journey of well-being and experience the metamorphosis of your life, achieving balance, purpose, and joy. *The Metamorphosis of Well-being: Synchronizing Wellness, Financial Stability, and Emotional Depth* is your ultimate guide to holistic well-being, offering practical tools and wisdom to create a life rich in health, security, and emotional depth.

www.ingramcontent.com/pod-product-compliance
Lightning Source LLC
Chambersburg PA
CBHW050156130526
44590CB00044B/3367